LOCH NESS MONSTER

PICTURE WINDOW BOOKS
a capstone imprint

Mythical Creatures is published by
Picture Window Books, an imprint of Capstone.
1710 Roe Crest Drive
North Mankato, Minnesota 56003
capstonepub.com

Library of Congress Cataloging-in-Publication Data
Names: Salazar, Alicia, 1973- author. | Calle, Juan, 1977- illustrator.
Title: Loch Ness monster / Alicia Salazar ; illustrated by Juan Calle.
Description: North Mankato, Minnesota : Picture Window Books, an imprint of
Capstone, [2022] | Includes bibliographical references. | Audience: Ages 5–7 |
Audience: Grades K–1 | Summary: "Look carefully! A dark shadow moves through the lapping lake water.
It's the Loch Ness Monster! This shy beast hides away from humans and treats lake dwellers
with kindness. Ever wondered about Nessie's diet and other habits? Does the lake monster
have companions? Wonder no more! Striking illustrations and matter-of-fact text take you on an
underwater journey to learn all about the Loch Ness Monster."— Provided by publisher.
Identifiers: LCCN 2021006165 (print) | LCCN 2021006166 (ebook) |
ISBN 9781663909664 (hardcover) | ISBN 9781663909633 (pdf) |
ISBN 9781663909657 (kindle edition)
Subjects: LCSH: Loch Ness monster—Juvenile literature.
Classification: LCC QL89.2.L6 S245 2022 (print) | LCC QL89.2.L6 (ebook) |
DDC 001.944—dc23
LC record available at https://lccn.loc.gov/2021006165
LC ebook record available at https://lccn.loc.gov/2021006166
Editor: Julie Gassman
Designer: Hilary Wacholz

Printed and bound in the USA. 004270

LOCH NESS MONSTER

by Alicia Salazar

illustrated by Juan Calle (Liberum Donum)

colors by Juan Calle and Luis Suarez

A quiet lake sits in the mountains of the Scottish Highlands. At 754 feet (230 meters) deep, Loch Ness is one of the deepest and largest lakes in Scotland. The surface is peaceful. A fisher's boat here. A fish jumping there.

But legend has it that a gentle beast swims deep beneath the surface.
The creature is known all around the world as the Loch Ness Monster.

LOCH NESS MONSTER BEHAVIOR

Sometimes called Nessie, the mythical animal stays away from humans. Only a few people have claimed to see her. People call her a monster because she is enormous, and they fear she might bite them or eat them. But Nessie doesn't eat people. She sticks to things like fish, clams, and snails.

Nessie spends most of her time in the deepest part of the lake.
But she breathes air and has to come up for oxygen between dives.

Nessie is an expert at hiding from humans. She only comes up when she knows no one is looking. She is also a very fast swimmer. She can get to the other side of the lake as fast as a cheetah can run.

Only one Loch Ness Monster has been seen at any one time. However, some people say that there is a family of monsters in the lake. Witnesses could be seeing a different one every time.

LIFE CYCLE OF A LOCH NESS MONSTER

Nessie was seen for the first time about 1,500 years ago. Many people think she is the last surviving dinosaur. Since dinosaurs lived 65 million years ago, it is unlikely any one animal could live that long. That's why some people think a number of different monsters must have lived in Loch Ness over the years.

YOUNG LOCH NESS

BABY LOCH NESS

ADULT LOCH NESS

No one has ever seen a Loch Ness Monster baby. But it is likely that each lake monster hatches from an egg, much like dinosaurs did. Then, the baby grows up to be a brand-new famous Loch Ness Monster.

LOCH NESS MONSTER FEATURES

People have only seen the Loch Ness Monster from the neck up. Blurry photos show a long neck rising out of the water, with a small head on top. Her head and neck look like that of a type of dinosaur called a plesiosaur.

PLESIOSAUR

LOCH NESS

Some witnesses say the rest of Nessie's body looks like a plesiosaur as well.
The average plesiosaur was about 11 feet (3.4 m) and 990 pounds (449 kilograms).
Nessie is a large creature too. She might be up to 15 feet (4.6 m) long.

Others claim that Nessie is a long serpent with a snake-like body. As she swims, her body goes in and out of the water, looking like three humps.

PARTS OF THE LOCK NESS MONSTER

EYES
She has two small, black eyes, one on each side of the head.

HEAD
Nessie's head is small and shaped like a snake's.

NOSTRILS
Two holes sit near the end of the snout. They are used to breathe in air when Nessie comes to the surface.

TEETH
Sharp, pointed teeth are used to pry open clams and snails.

LONG NECK
Nessie's neck is at least 5 feet (1.5 m) long. It can be seen in photographs reaching out of the water in the most famous pictures of Nessie.

DORSAL HUMP

If Nessie looks like a plesiosaur, she has one large hump. If she looks like a serpent, her hump or humps could be an illusion caused by her moving in and out of the water as she swims.

TAIL

Nessie's long, pointy tail helps her turn her body while she is swimming.

FLIPPERS

Nessie's flippers help her swim. They look like four large oars where her legs would be.

LOCH NESS MONSTER OF MYTH

Legend says that the first sighting of the Loch Ness Monster was in 567 AD by Columba. He was an Irish man who later became a saint. He stopped the creature from attacking a swimmer by saying to Nessie, "Go back!"

The first photograph of the Loch Ness Monster was taken in 1933. Hugh Gray, an amateur photographer, took the photo after hearing reports of a Nessie sighting. Some people said they saw a large creature with no limbs cross the road. Others reported they saw a creature with flippers crossing the road and diving into the loch.

Many humans have tried to find Nessie. In 1972, two boats set out on Loch Ness with time-lapse cameras attached underneath. The team came back with a photo of a large flipper.

LAKE MONSTERS AROUND THE WORLD

Lake monsters are rumored to live all around the world. Just like with Nessie, humans try to catch a peek at them.

LAKE VAN MONSTER

Lake Van, Turkey
Measures about 49 feet (15 m)
long with spikes on its back

OGOPOGO

Okanagan Lake, Canada
Rises out of the water and
eats things as large as horses

STORSJÖODJURET

Lake Storsjön, Sweden
A snake-like creature with
humps and a small head

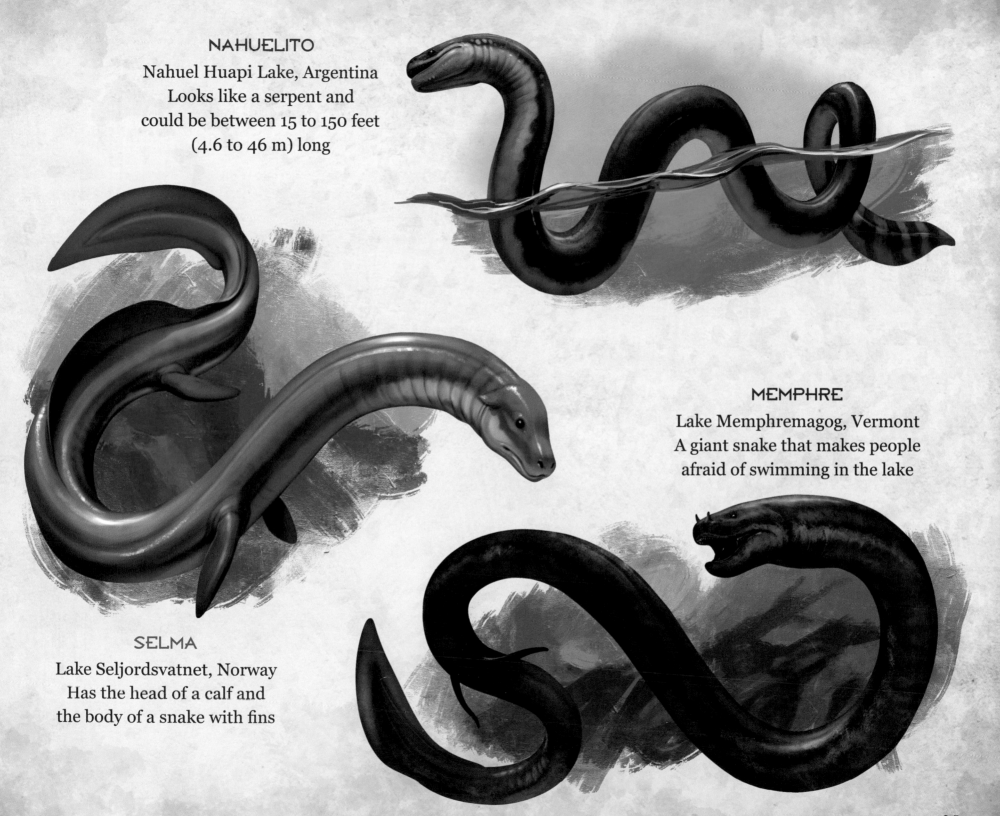

NAHUELITO
Nahuel Huapi Lake, Argentina
Looks like a serpent and
could be between 15 to 150 feet
(4.6 to 46 m) long

MEMPHRE
Lake Memphremagog, Vermont
A giant snake that makes people
afraid of swimming in the lake

SELMA
Lake Seljordsvatnet, Norway
Has the head of a calf and
the body of a snake with fins

Whether Nessie is one creature in a group or she lives on her own, she continues to live hidden from the prying eyes of humans. People will always wonder about her and watch for her in Loch Ness.

But remember, it takes a lot of dedication to actually see her. Some people spend many years trying and never do. If you find yourself at the shoreline of the Scottish lake, keep a watchful eye. You may be one of the lucky ones.

ABOUT THE AUTHOR

Alicia Salazar is a Mexican American children's book author who has written for blogs, magazines, and education publishers. She was also once an elementary school teacher and a marine biologist. She currently lives in the suburbs of Houston, Texas, but is a city girl at heart. When she is not dreaming up new adventures to experience, she is turning her adventures into stories for kids.

ABOUT THE ILLUSTRATOR

Juan Calle is a former biologist turned science illustrator, trained at the Science Illustration program at California State University, Monterey Bay. Early on in his illustration career, he worked on field guides of plants and animals native to his country of origin, Colombia. Now he owns and works in his art studio, Liberum Donum, creating concept art, storyboards, and his passion: comic books.

GLOSSARY

amateur—someone who does something as a hobby, rather than to earn money

behavior—the way a person or animal acts

dedication—the act of giving time, effort, and attention to something

dorsal hump—a hump located on the back of an animal

enormous—very large

illusion—something that appears to be real but isn't

mythical—based on stories from ancient times

oxygen—a gas that people and some animals breathe in order to live

plesiosaur—a large swimming reptile that lived during the time of the dinosaurs

prying—looking or searching curiously

serpent—a snake

witness—a person who has seen or heard something

CRITICAL THINKING QUESTIONS

1. Based on what you've read, would you be afraid to come face to face with the Loch Ness Monster? Why or why not?

2. There are stories of lake monsters all over the world, but the Loch Ness Monster is by far the most famous. Why do you think that is?

3. Using a book or internet site, learn more about the plesiosaur. (Ask a grown-up for help, if needed.) In what ways is Nessie similar to a plesiosaur?

READ MORE

Olson, Gillia M. *Curious about the Loch Ness Monster*. Mankato, MN: Amicus, 2021.

Ranson, Candice F. *Mysterious Loch Ness Monster*. Minneapolis: Lerner Publications, 2021.

Troupe, Thomas Kingsley. *Searching for the Loch Ness Monster*. Minneapolis: Bellwether Media, 2021.

INTERNET SITES

Loch Ness Monster Facts for Kids
kids.kiddle.co/Loch_Ness_Monster

Nessie, the Loch Ness Monster
learnenglishkids.britishcouncil.org/short-stories/nessie-the-loch-ness-monster

READ THEM ALL!

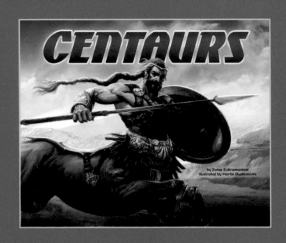

CENTAURS

by Suma Subramaniam
Illustrated by Martin Bustamante

DRAGONS

by Matt Doeden
Illustrated by Martin Bustamante

FAIRIES

by Suma Subramaniam
Illustrated by Martin Bustamante

GRIFFINS

BY MATT DOEDEN
ILLUSTRATED BY MARTIN BUSTAMANTE

LOCH NESS MONSTER

by Alicia Salazar
Illustrated by Juan Calle

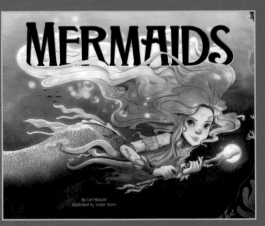

MERMAIDS

by Cari Meister
Illustrated by Xavier Bonet

TROLLS

by Alicia Salazar
Illustrated by Dan Whisker

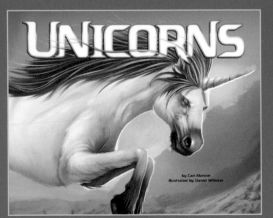

UNICORNS

by Cari Meister
Illustrated by Daniel Whisker